IT'S TIME TO COLORING

CONSTRUCTION MACHINES

Use crayons or a brush and paints

Enjoy your time :)

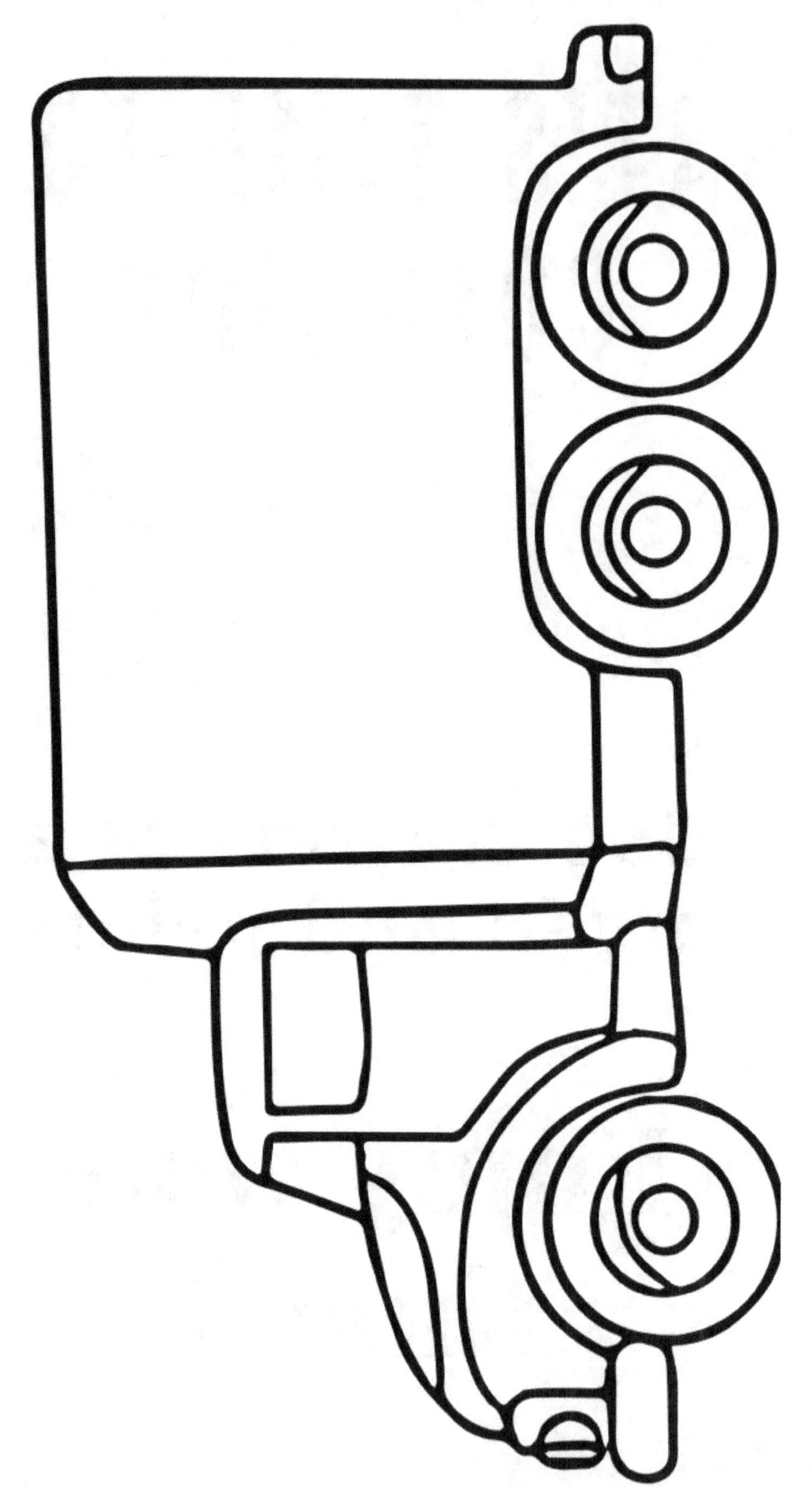

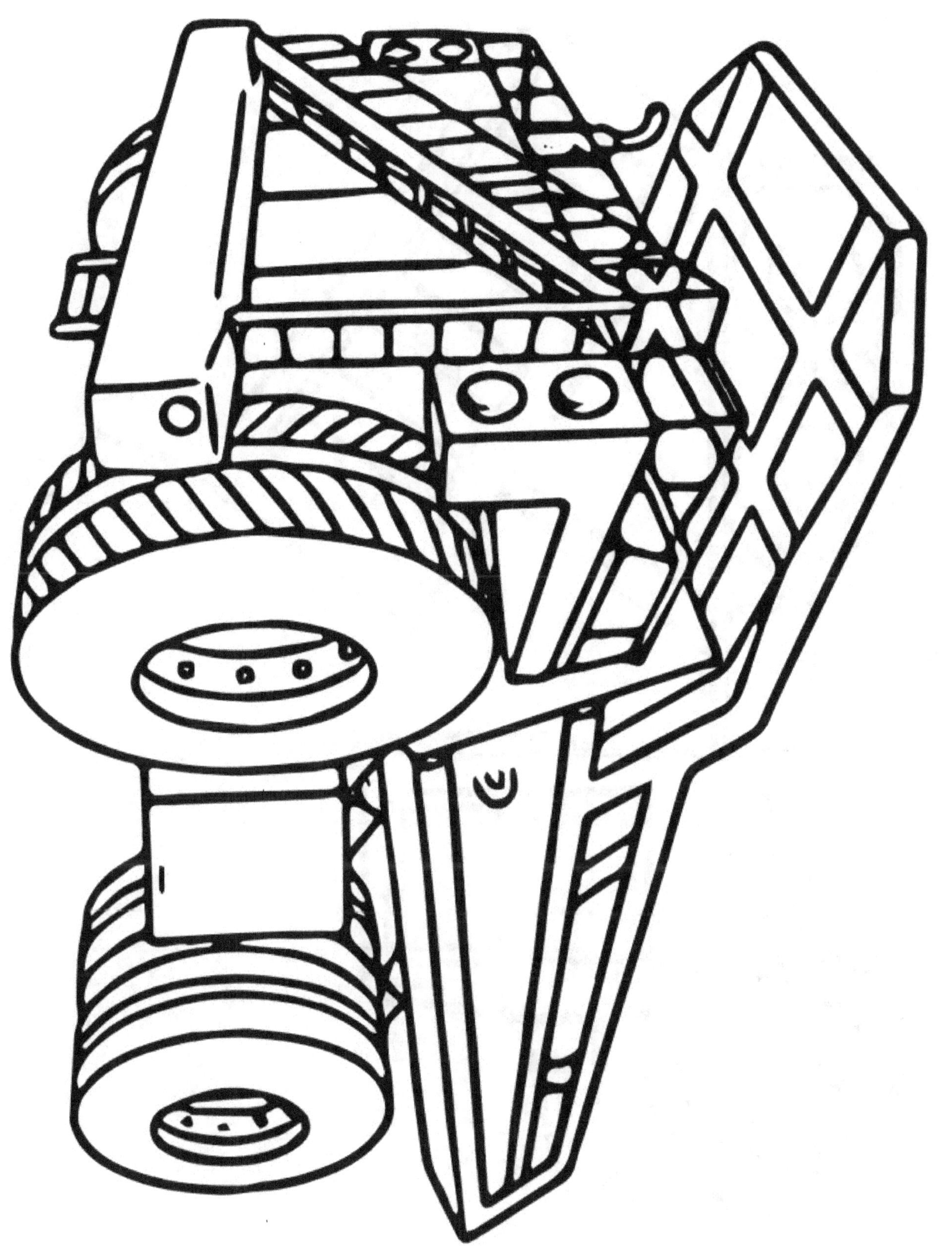

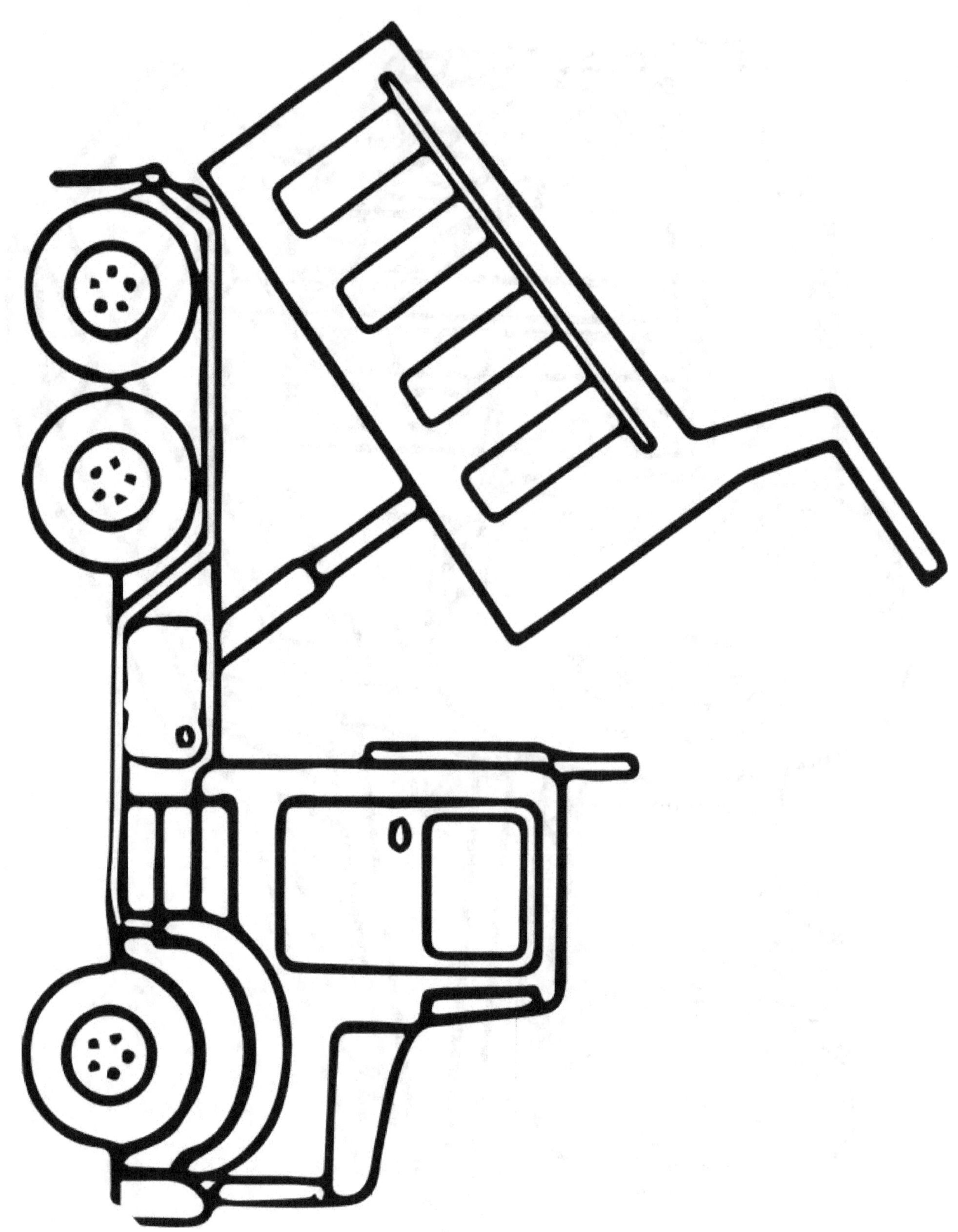

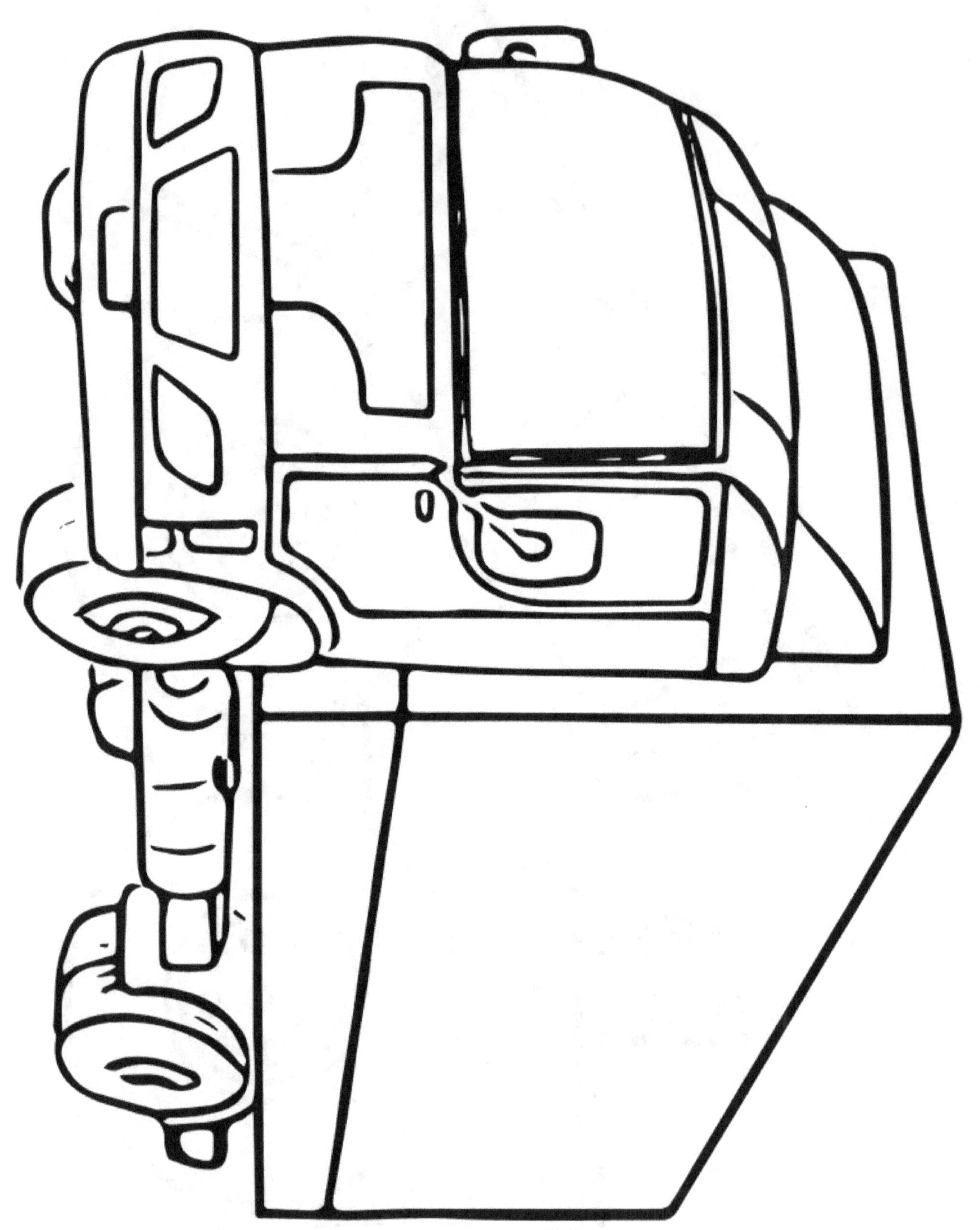

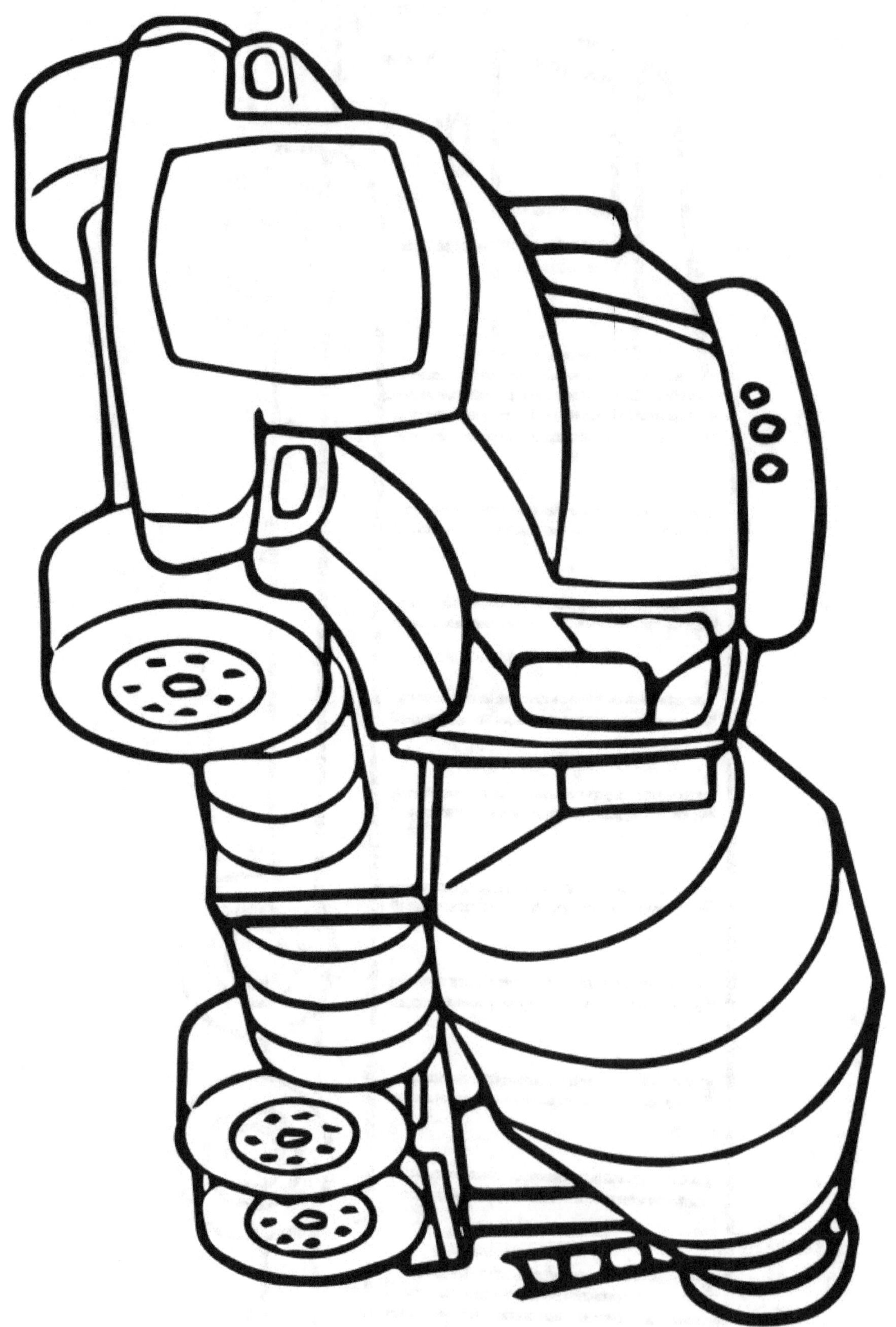

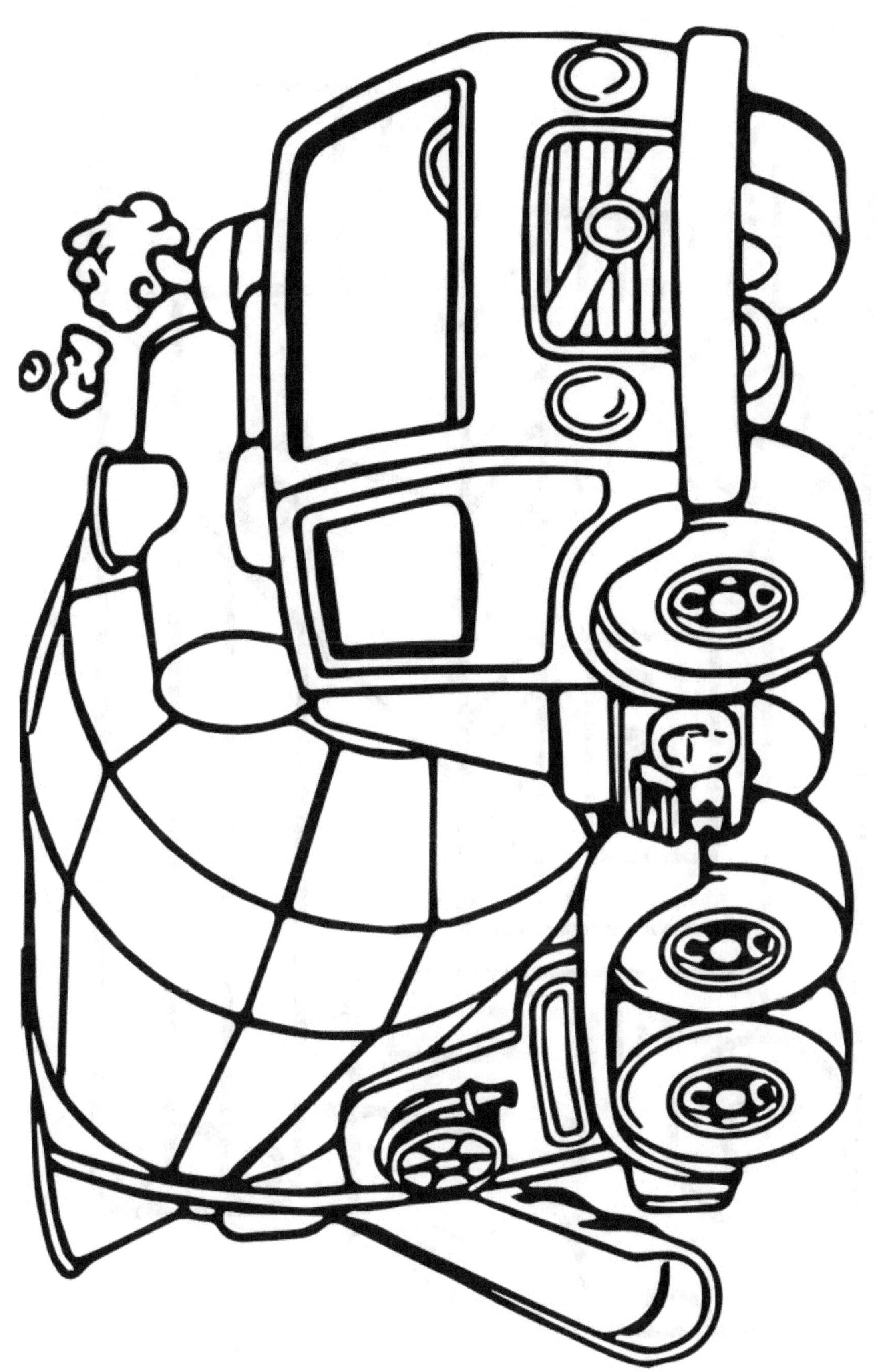

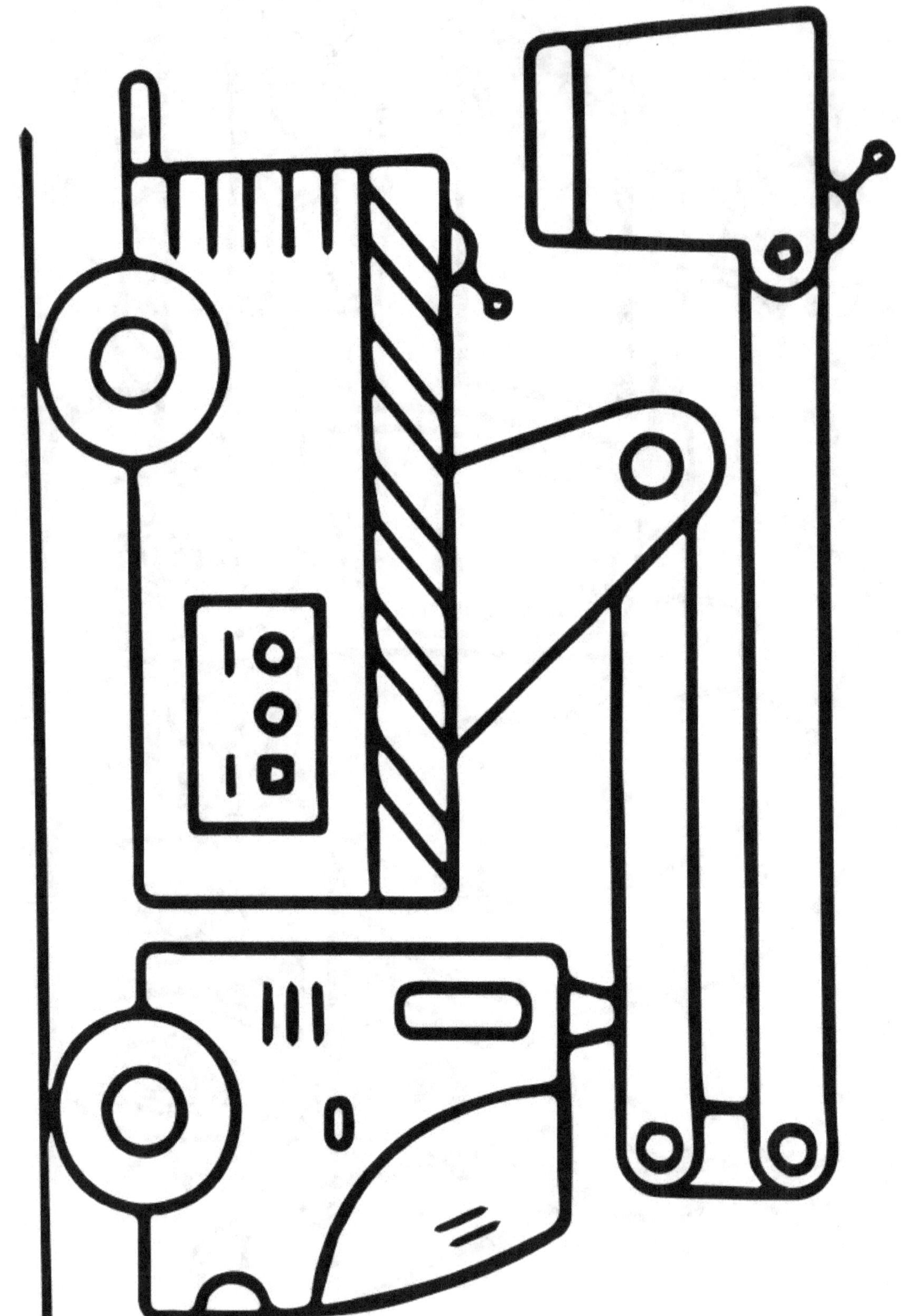

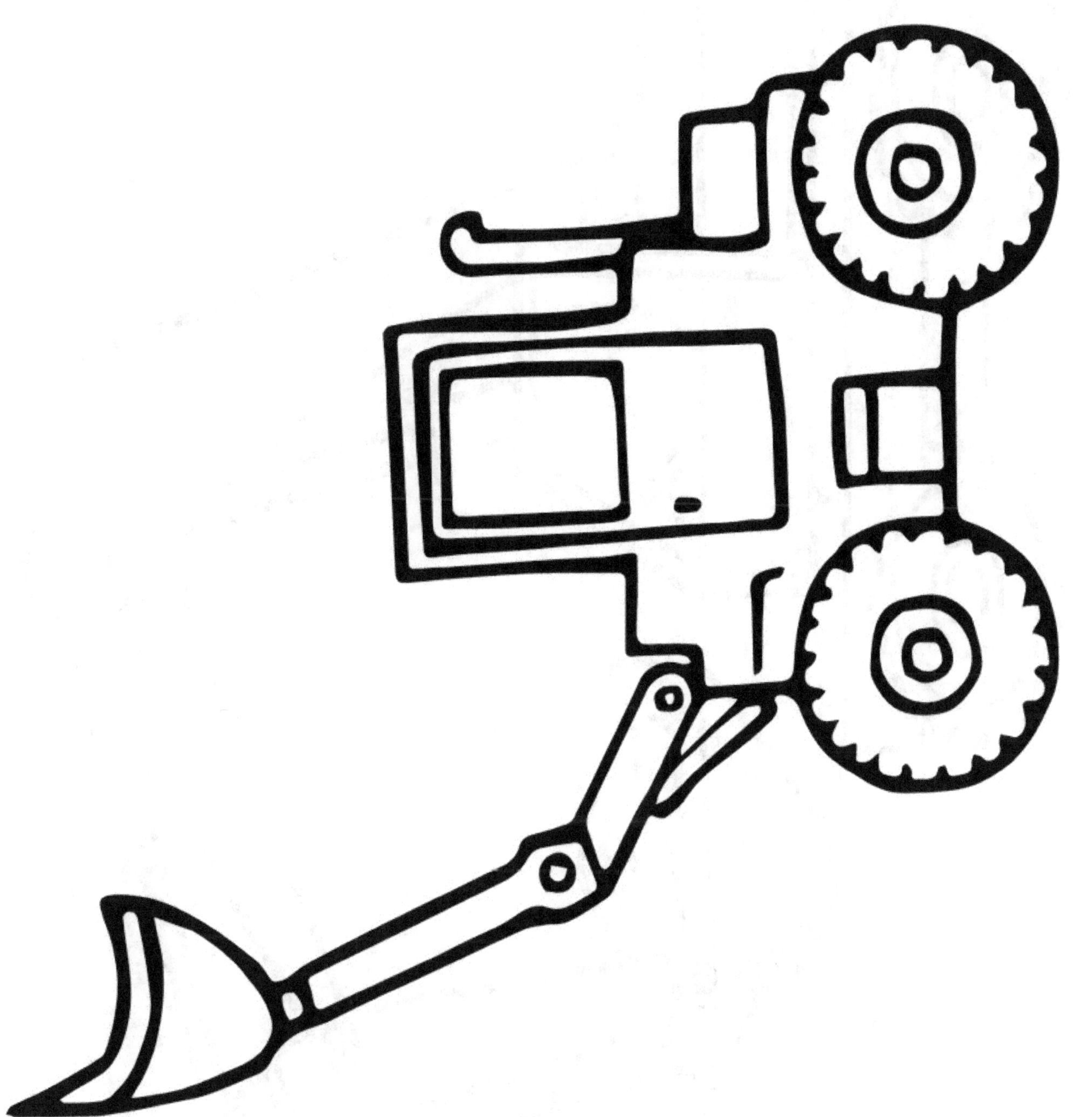

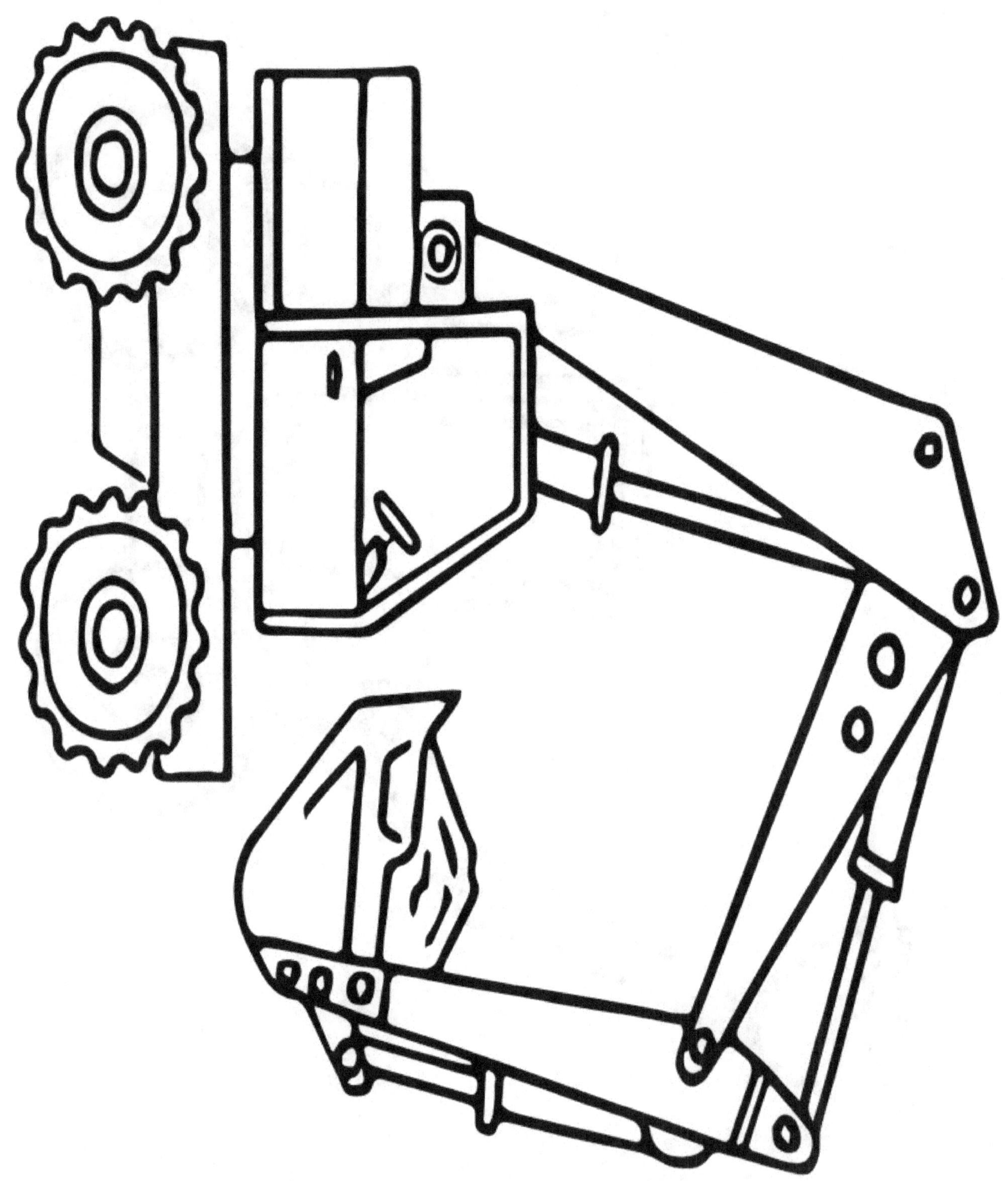

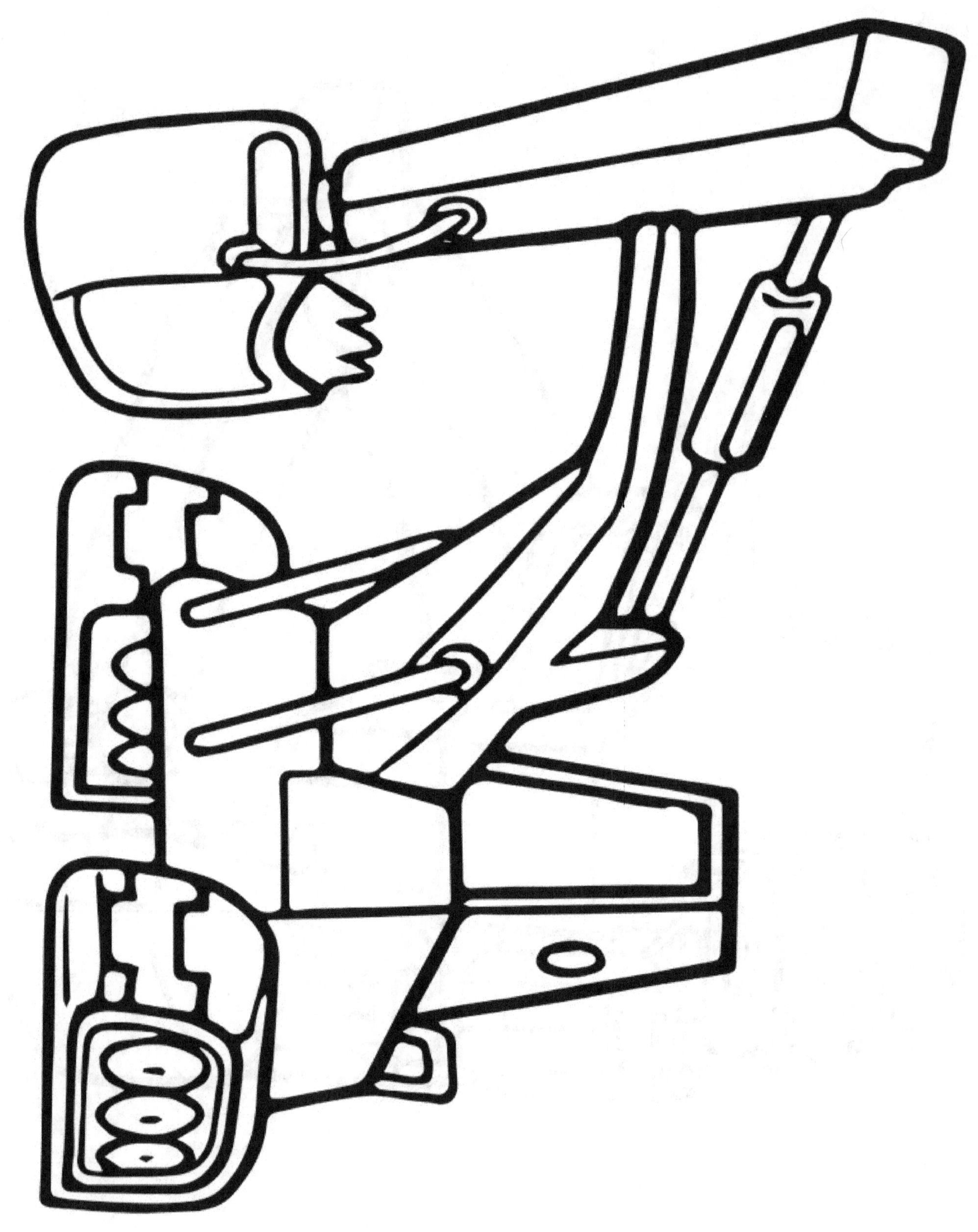

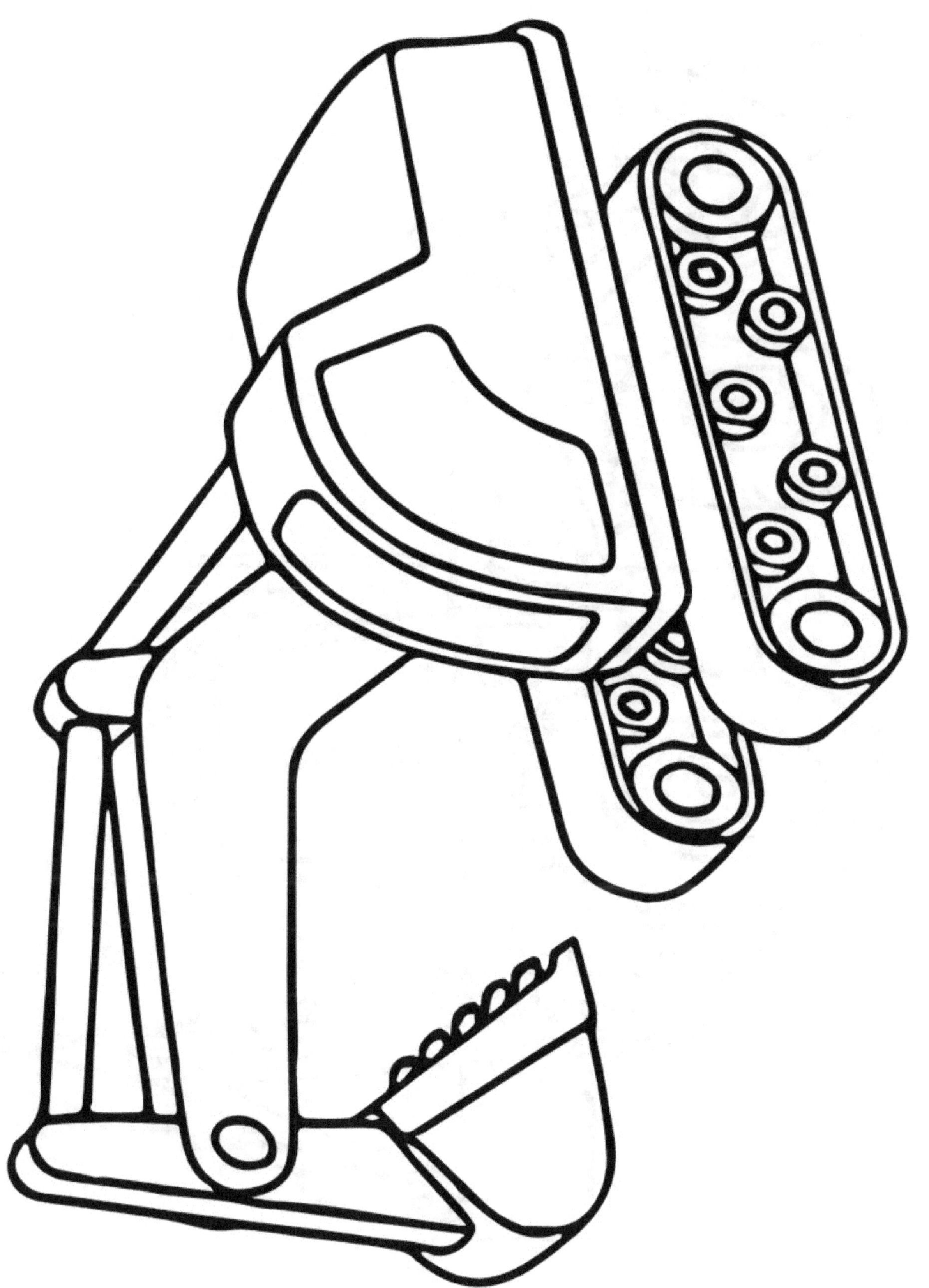

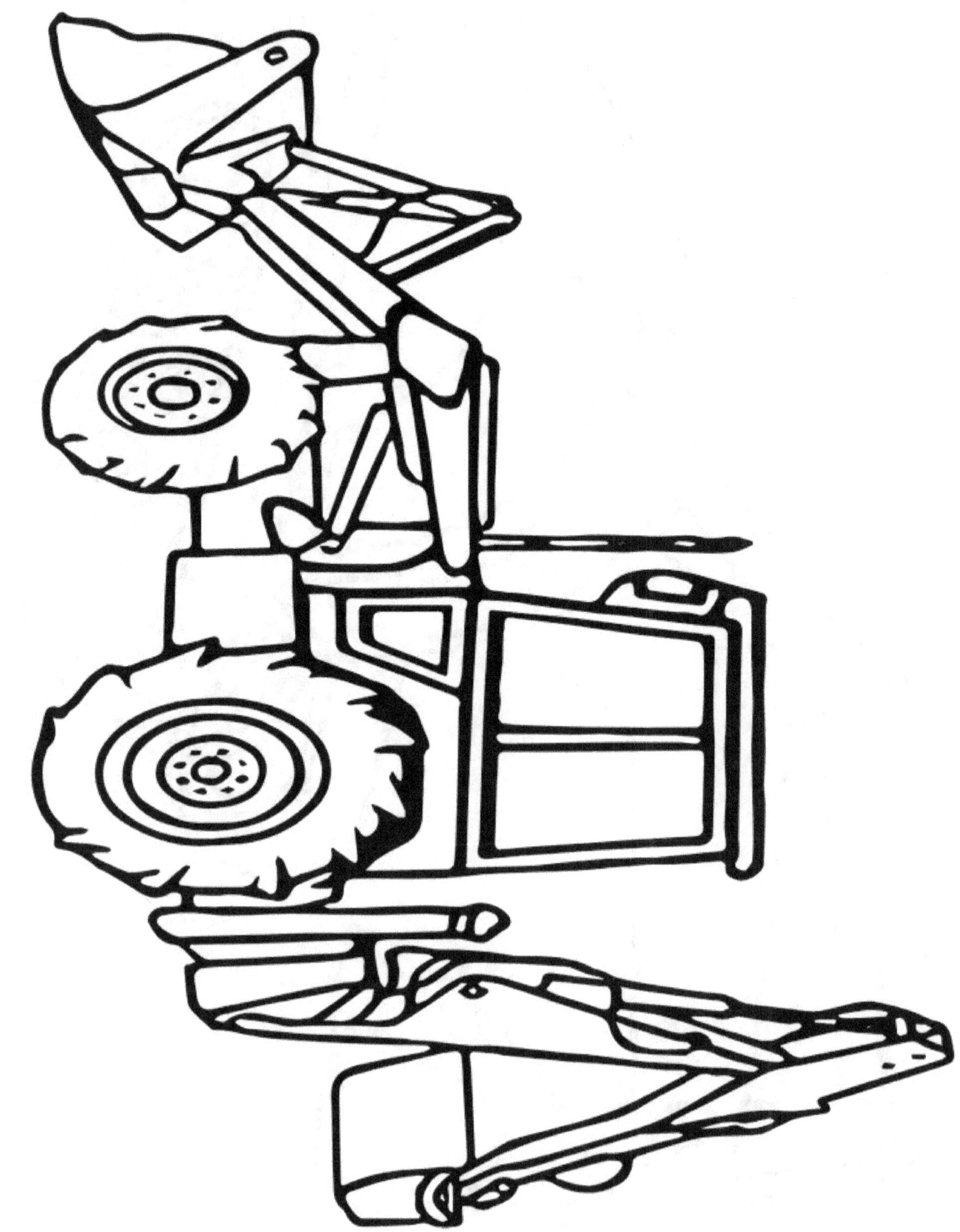

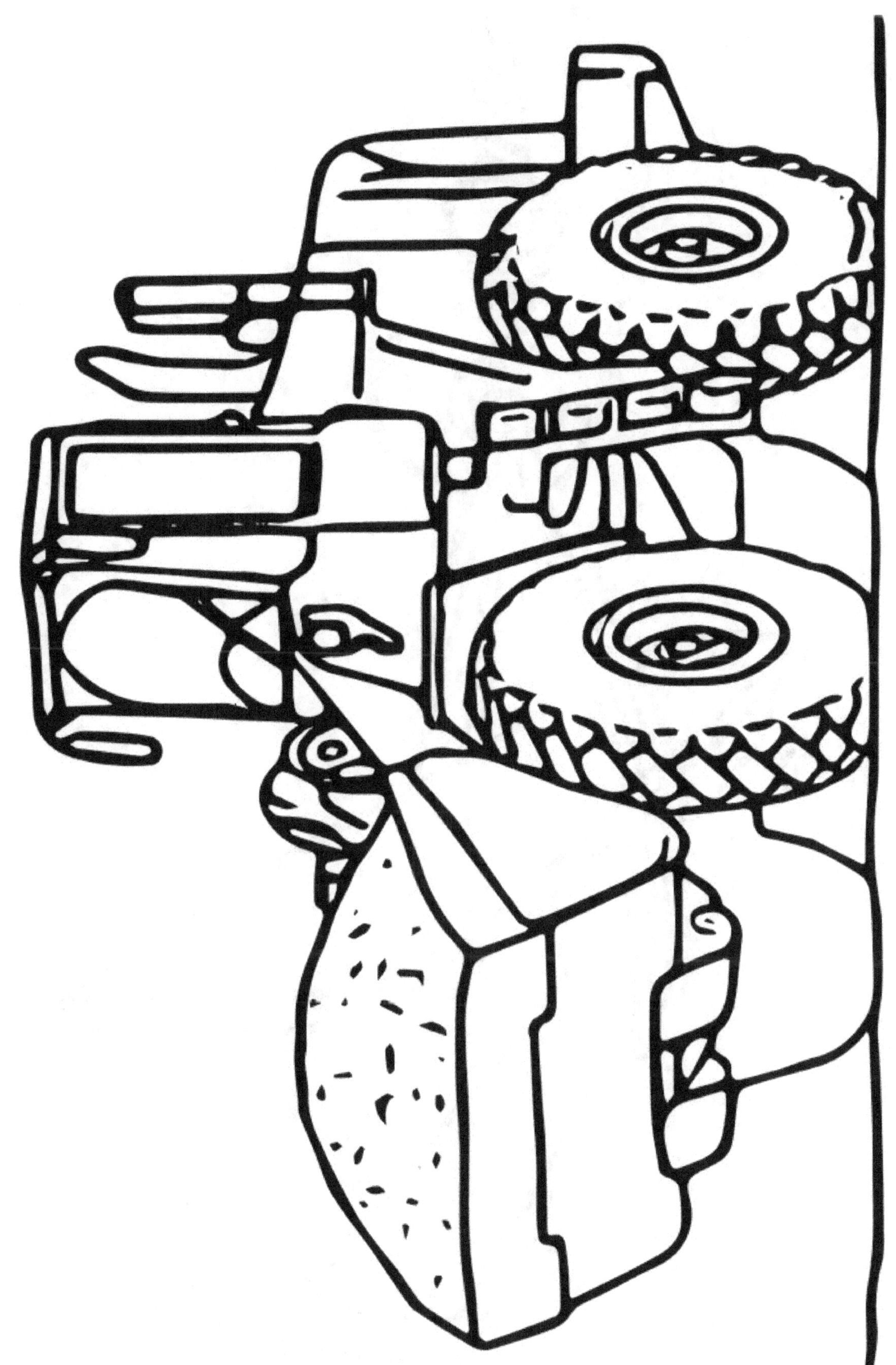

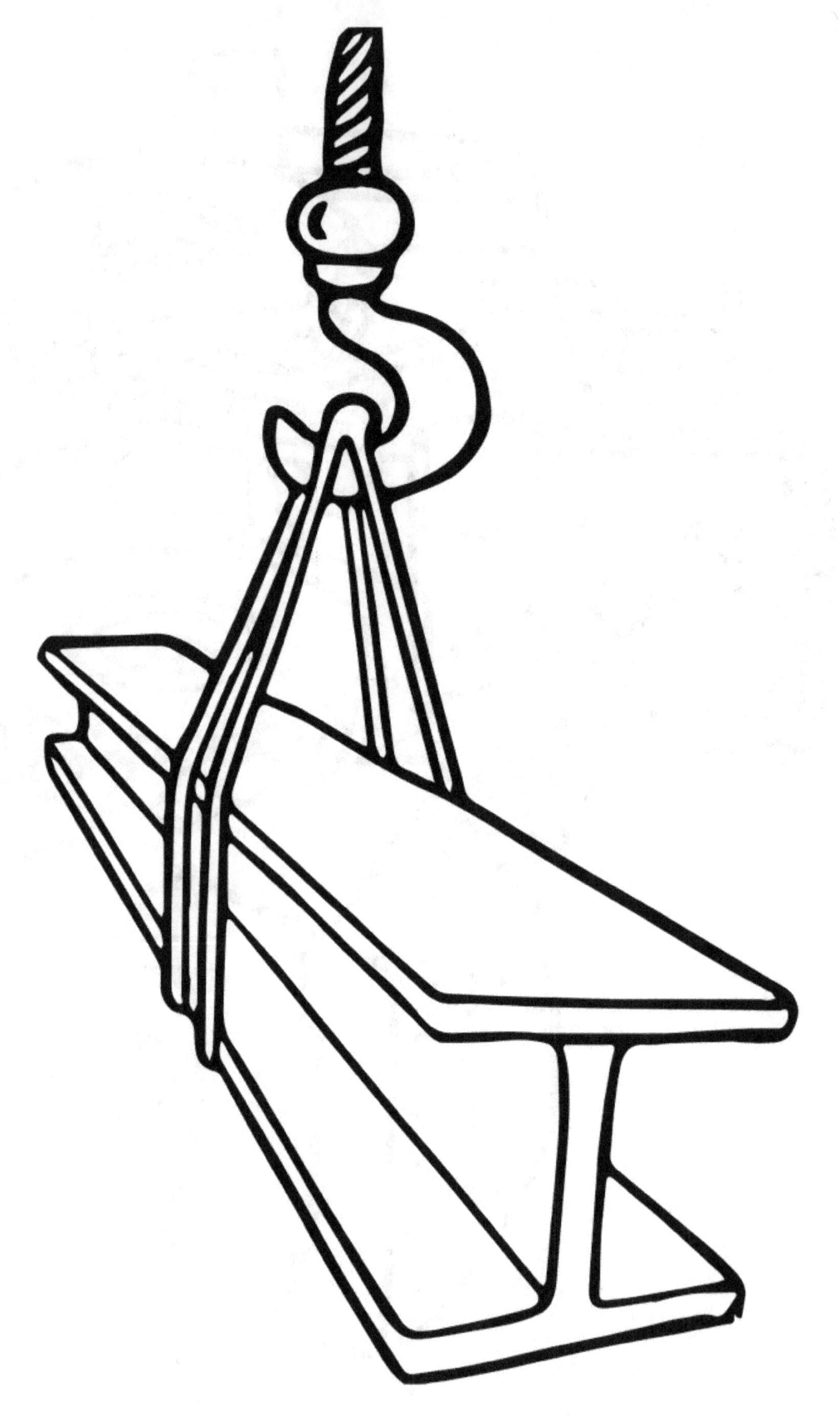

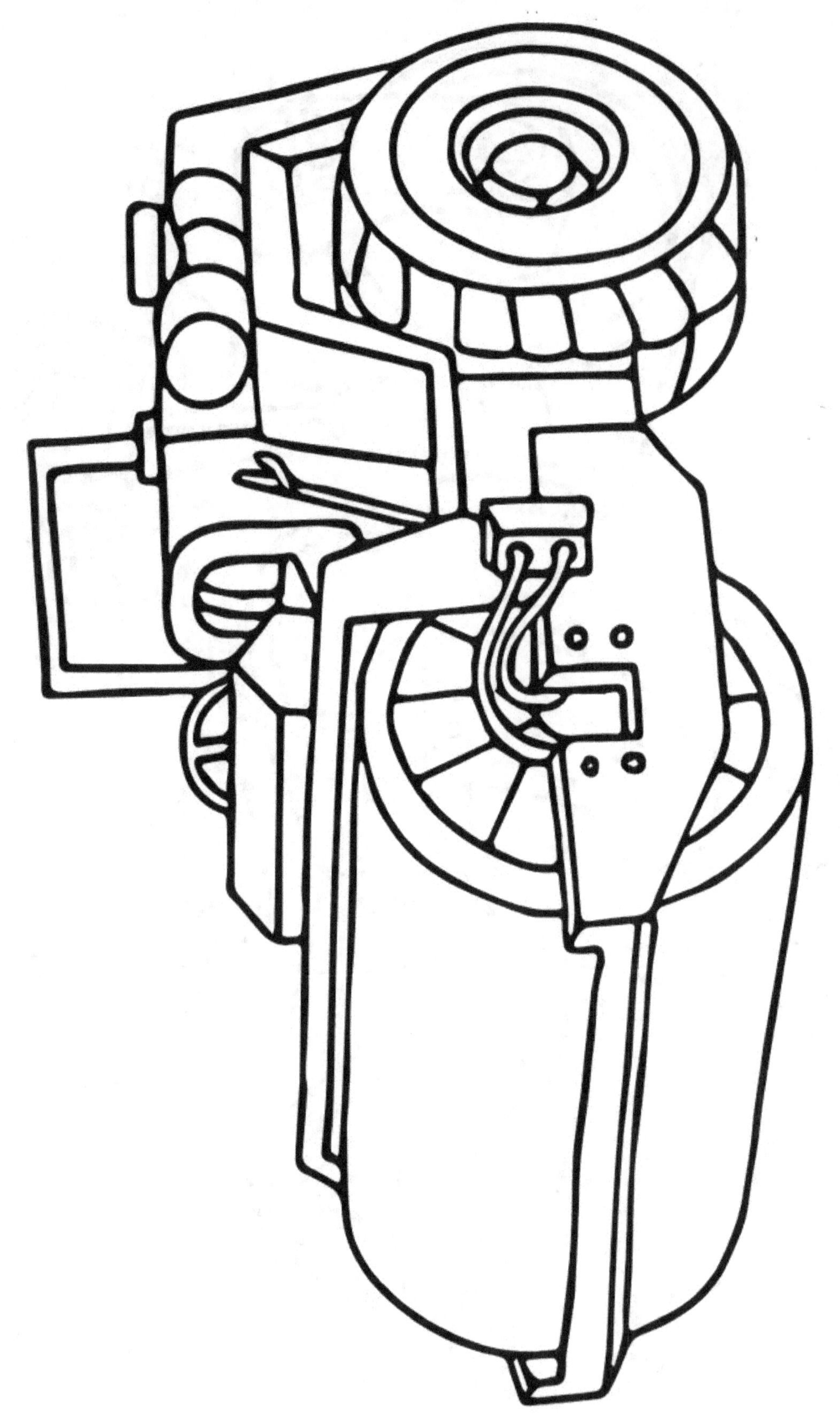

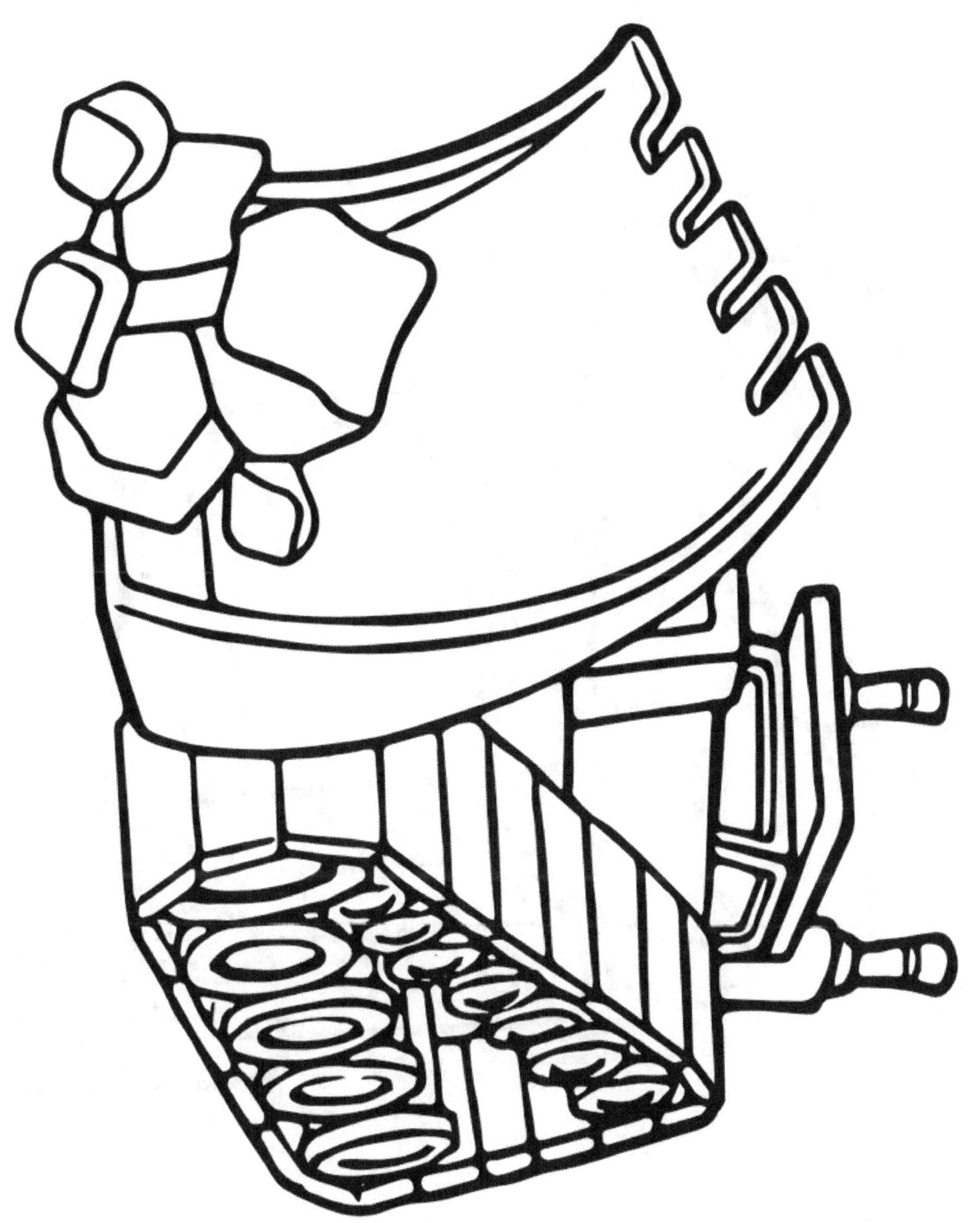

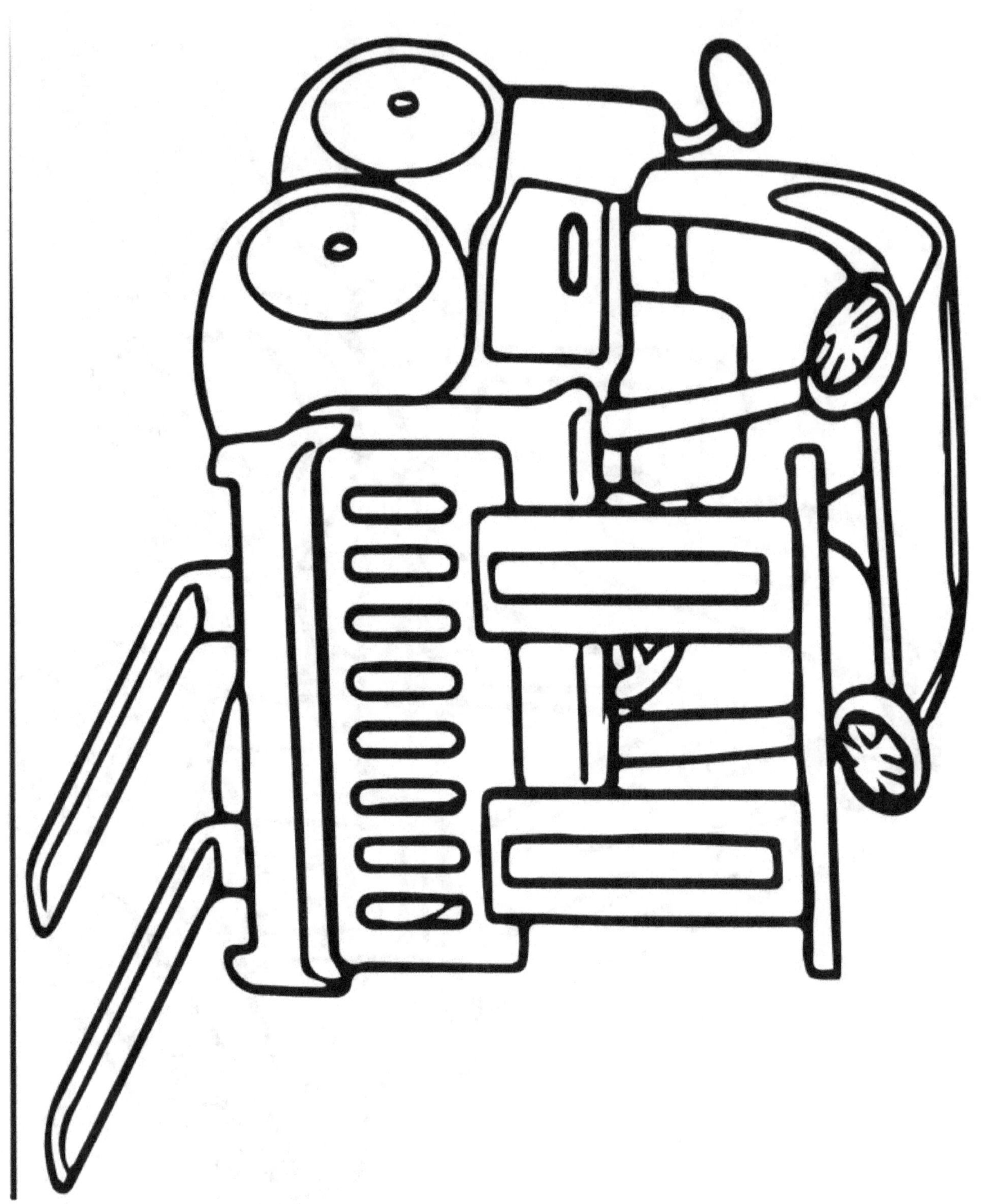

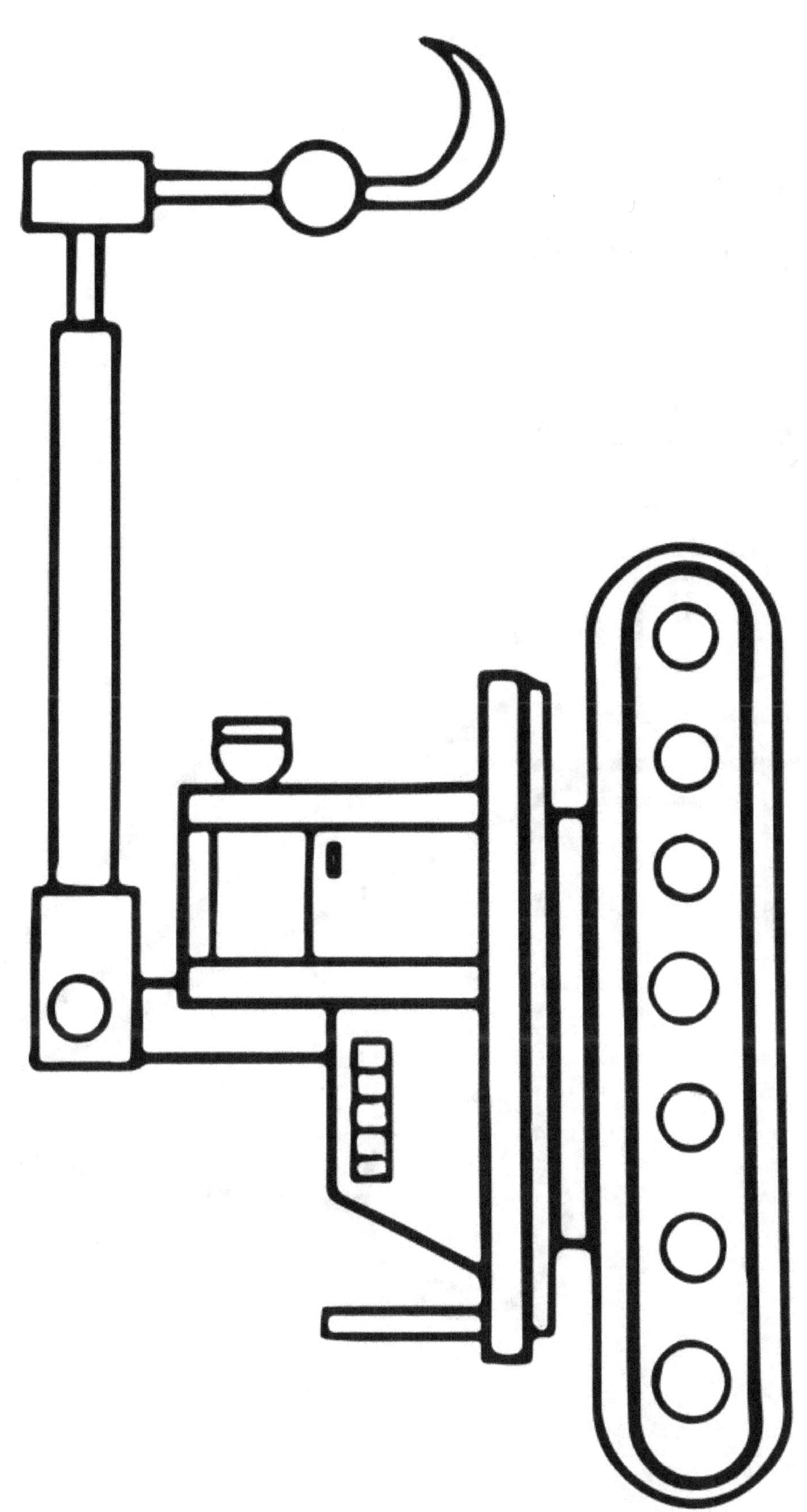

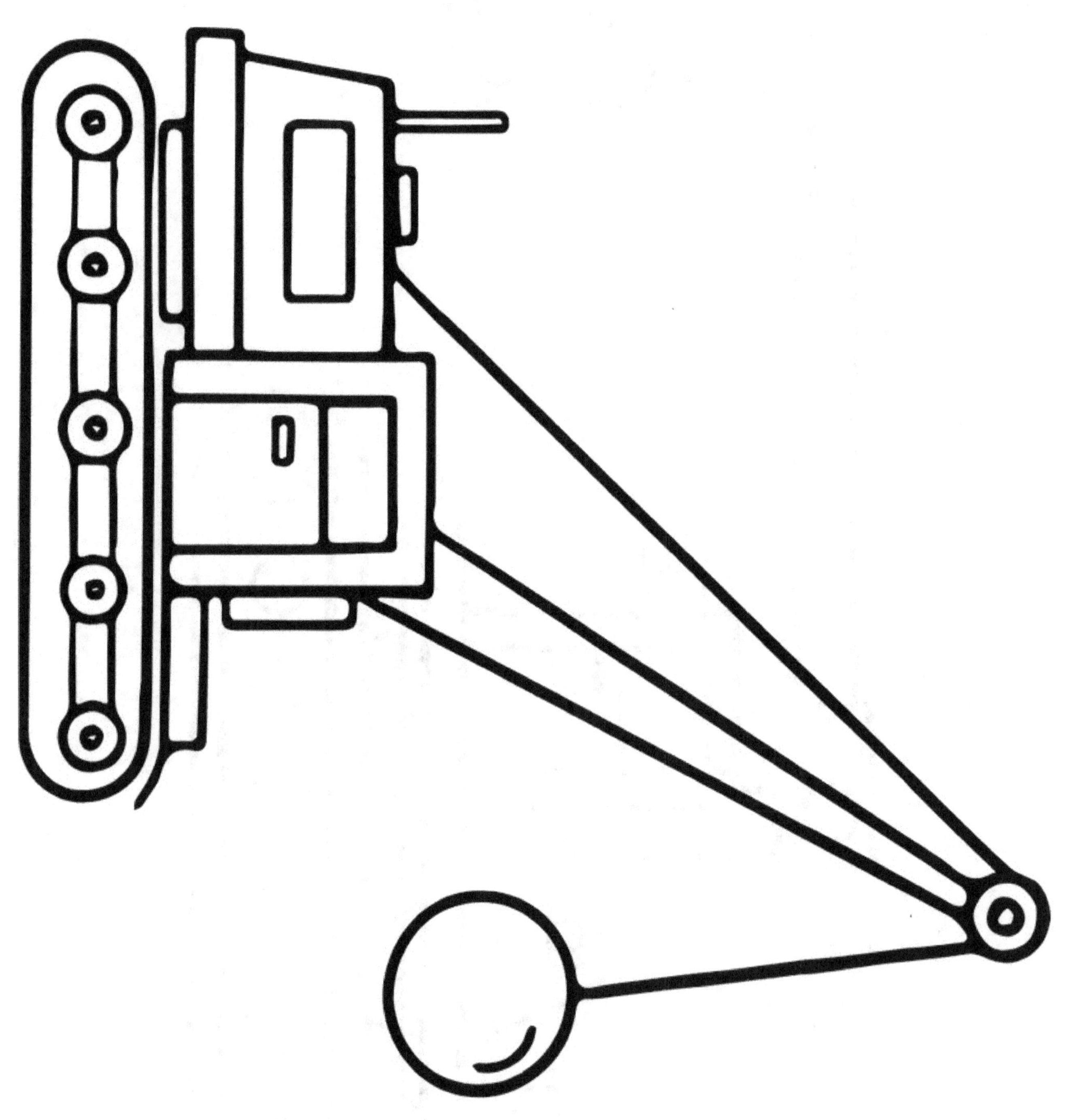

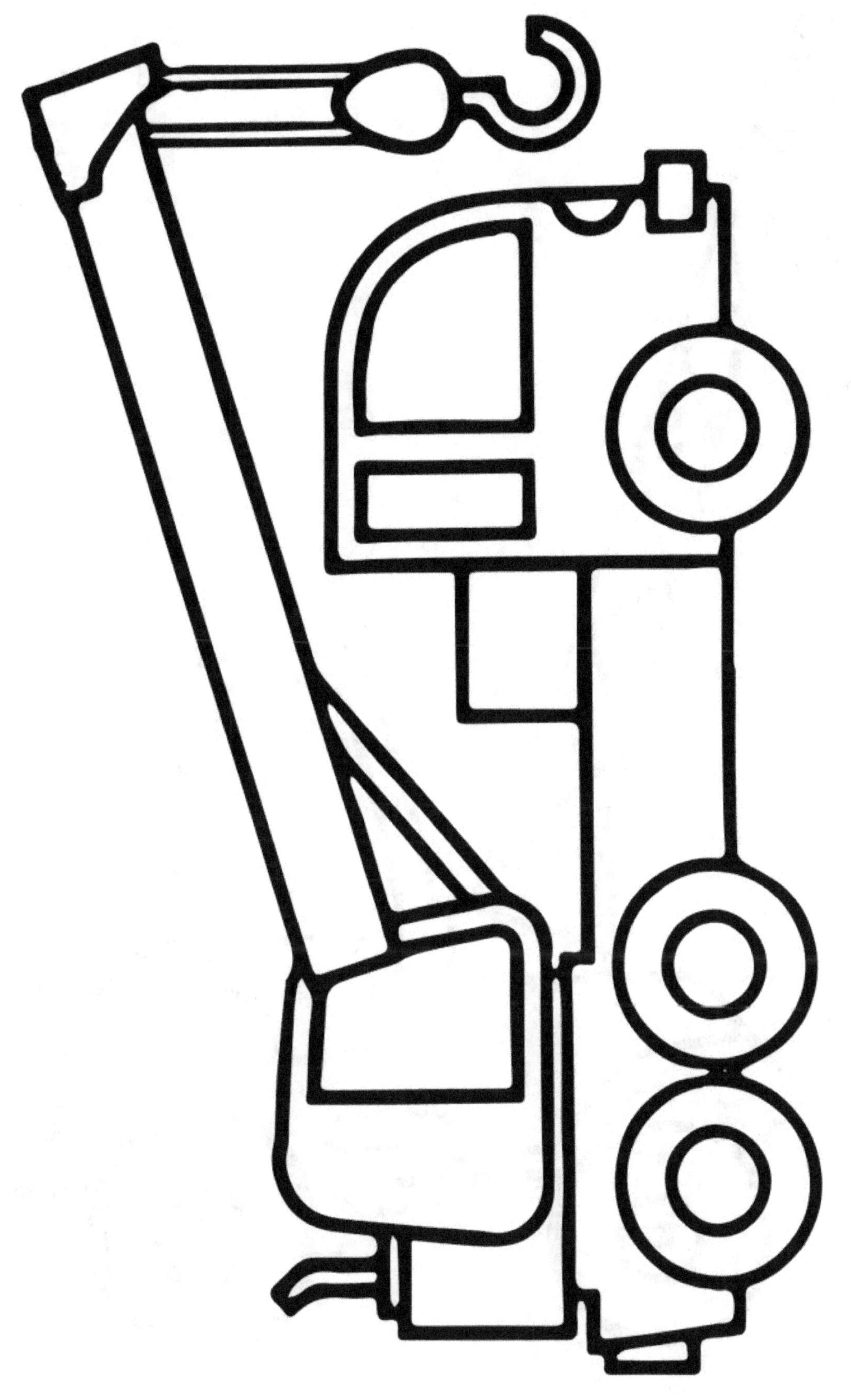

Thank you for purchasing my coloring book

I hope I have brought great joy to your child